PART A

PMP Exam – Set 1 (Questions 1-33)

People Domain

1. A key stakeholder is unhappy with the project's progress. What should the project manager do first?
    - A) Ignore the stakeholder and continue working
    - B) Escalate the issue to the sponsor
    - C) Meet with the stakeholder to understand their concerns
    - D) Assign a team member to handle the situation

2. During a project, a conflict arises between two team members. What is the best approach for the project manager to resolve the conflict?
    - A) Forcing a solution
    - B) Avoiding the conflict
    - C) Collaborating to find a win-win solution
    - D) Withdrawing from the conflict

3. Which leadership style focuses on guiding and mentoring team members to enhance their skills and abilities?
    - A) Laissez-faire
    - B) Autocratic
    - C) Coaching
    - D) Democratic

4. In an agile team, who is responsible for ensuring the team follows the process and removes impediments?
    - A) Product Owner
    - B) Scrum Master
    - C) Team Lead
    - D) Project Manager

5. A team is facing performance issues and low morale. According to Herzberg's Two-Factor Theory, which factor is most likely causing dissatisfaction?
    - A) Achievement

- B) Recognition
- C) Poor working conditions
- D) Personal growth

6. Which stage of team development is characterized by the highest level of productivity?
   - A) Forming
   - B) Storming
   - C) Norming
   - D) Performing

7. What is the best way to handle a low-power, high-interest stakeholder?
   - A) Keep them informed
   - B) Manage them closely
   - C) Monitor them with minimal effort
   - D) Keep them satisfied

8. Emotional intelligence in project management focuses on:
   - A) Controlling emotions at all times
   - B) Understanding and managing one's own and others' emotions
   - C) Avoiding emotional situations
   - D) Making decisions based solely on logic

9. A project team is working remotely, and communication issues are becoming a challenge. What should the project manager do?
   - A) Increase the frequency of meetings
   - B) Reduce the number of meetings
   - C) Implement a virtual collaboration tool
   - D) Avoid discussing communication issues

10. When providing feedback to a team member, what is the most effective approach?
    - A) Publicly criticize their work to set an example
    - B) Offer constructive criticism in private and suggest improvements
    - C) Ignore the issue

- D) Give generic praise without specifics

Process Domain

11. In earned value management (EVM), which formula is used to calculate cost performance index (CPI)?
    - A) CPI = EV / PV
    - B) CPI = EV / AC
    - C) CPI = AC / EV
    - D) CPI = BAC / EV

12. If a project has a CPI of 0.9, what does this indicate?
    - A) The project is under budget
    - B) The project is on budget
    - C) The project is over budget
    - D) The project is ahead of schedule

13. Which process is responsible for ensuring the project stays on schedule?
    - A) Control Scope
    - B) Control Schedule
    - C) Control Costs
    - D) Monitor Risks

14. A project team is tasked with delivering a new software product. The project manager defines activities, estimates their durations, and sequences them. What process is the project manager performing?
    - A) Define Activities
    - B) Develop Schedule
    - C) Plan Scope Management
    - D) Plan Schedule Management

15. What is the critical path in project management?
    - A) The shortest path through the project
    - B) The path with the least risk
    - C) The longest path through the project

- D) The path that involves the least amount of work

16. A project has a budget of $200,000 and is halfway through the timeline. The project has spent $100,000 so far and achieved only 40% of the planned work. What is the earned value (EV)?
    - A) $40,000
    - B) $80,000
    - C) $100,000
    - D) $120,000

17. What is a key benefit of performing a stakeholder analysis?
    - A) To identify potential risks
    - B) To develop a communication plan
    - C) To prioritize stakeholders based on their influence and interest
    - D) To create a project schedule

18. In risk management, what is the first step to address project risks?
    - A) Perform Qualitative Risk Analysis
    - B) Plan Risk Responses
    - C) Identify Risks
    - D) Monitor Risks

19. Which tool or technique is used to determine the root cause of a problem in quality management?
    - A) Fishbone Diagram
    - B) Pareto Chart
    - C) Control Chart
    - D) Gantt Chart

20. The sponsor requests changes to the project scope after the project plan has been approved. What should the project manager do first?
    - A) Refuse the change
    - B) Implement the change immediately
    - C) Evaluate the impact of the change and follow the change control process

- D) Ignore the request

Business Environment Domain

21. A new regulation is introduced that affects your project. What should the project manager do first?
    - A) Update the risk register
    - B) Conduct an impact analysis
    - C) Inform the project sponsor
    - D) Cancel the project

22. In a project, the project manager realizes that the objectives are no longer aligned with the business goals due to market changes. What should the project manager do?
    - A) Continue the project as planned
    - B) Request additional funding to realign objectives
    - C) Recommend terminating the project
    - D) Adjust project objectives to align with the new goals

23. The project manager is working on a project that involves multiple external vendors. Which contract type transfers the most risk to the seller?
    - A) Cost-Reimbursable Contract
    - B) Fixed-Price Contract
    - C) Time and Materials Contract
    - D) Cost Plus Incentive Fee Contract

24. What is benefits realization in project management?
    - A) Tracking project deliverables
    - B) Ensuring that the project's outcomes deliver the intended value to the organization
    - C) Monitoring project risks
    - D) Closing the project

25. Which organizational structure allows the project manager to have the most authority over project decisions?

- A) Functional
- B) Weak Matrix
- C) Balanced Matrix
- D) Projectized

Agile and Hybrid

26. In an agile project, what is a sprint retrospective focused on?
    - A) Delivering product features
    - B) Reviewing completed work
    - C) Identifying process improvements
    - D) Adjusting the project scope

27. In a hybrid project, the team is using predictive techniques for certain parts and agile for others. Which factor should the project manager consider when tailoring the approach?
    - A) The project team's preferences
    - B) Stakeholder communication needs
    - C) The project budget
    - D) The weather

28. A Scrum team conducts a sprint review. What is the primary focus of this meeting?
    - A) Discussing project risks
    - B) Demonstrating the work completed during the sprint
    - C) Planning the next sprint
    - D) Revisiting the project schedule

29. What is the role of a Product Owner in an agile project?
    - A) Developing the project schedule
    - B) Defining and prioritizing the product backlog
    - C) Facilitating the daily standup meetings
    - D) Managing the project team

30. In agile methodologies, what does "time-boxed" refer to?

- A) The duration of meetings
- B) The fixed time allocated for completing an activity or task
- C) The number of team members involved in an activity
- D) The cost constraint of the project

Ethics and Professional Conduct

31. A project manager is offered a gift by a vendor during a project. According to PMI's Code of Ethics, what should the project manager do?
    - A) Accept the gift if it benefits the project
    - B) Politely decline the gift
    - C) Accept the gift and report it to the sponsor
    - D) Accept the gift only if it's below a certain value

32. How should a project manager handle sensitive project information that could impact the project's success?
    - A) Share it with the entire team to maintain transparency
    - B) Keep it confidential and share it only with authorized stakeholders
    - C) Ignore the information to avoid conflict
    - D) Share it publicly to prevent any misunderstandings

33. A team member approaches the project manager with concerns about unethical practices within the project. What should the project manager do?
    - A) Investigate the concerns and take appropriate action
    - B) Dismiss the concerns to avoid conflict
    - C) Report the issue directly to the project sponsor
    - D) Encourage the team member to ignore the issue

Answers for Set 1 (Questions 1–33)

1. C
2. C
3. C
4. B
5. C
6. D
7. A
8. B
9. C
10. B
11. B
12. C
13. B
14. A
15. C
16. A
17. C
18. C
19. A
20. C
21. B
22. D
23. B
24. B
25. D
26. C
27. B
28. B
29. B
30. B
31. B
32. B
33. A

PMP Exam - Set 2 (Questions 34-66)

People Domain

34. A project manager is assigning tasks to team members based on their strengths and expertise. Which leadership style is the project manager demonstrating?
- A) Autocratic
- B) Transformational
- C) Transactional
- D) Delegative

35. A project manager notices that one of the team members has not been contributing as expected. How should the project manager address this?
- A) Ignore the issue and hope the team member improves
- B) Assign more work to the team member to motivate them
- C) Meet with the team member privately to understand and resolve the issue
- D) Report the team member to HR for underperformance

36. When working with a virtual team, what is the most effective strategy to maintain team cohesion?
- A) Limit meetings to avoid over-communication
- B) Use regular video conferencing and team-building activities
- C) Focus on individual assignments rather than team collaboration
- D) Provide daily email updates to the team

37. Which is the most important responsibility of a project manager when managing a diverse project team?
- A) Focus on the team's personal relationships
- B) Ensure that all team members respect and value diversity
- C) Minimize conflicts by separating diverse team members
- D) Delegate leadership tasks to others

38. A stakeholder has been identified as high-power, low-interest. How should the project manager handle this stakeholder?
- A) Keep them informed regularly

- B) Monitor them closely with little effort
- C) Keep them satisfied
- D) Engage them directly in the project

39. During a project meeting, two team members are having a heated argument. What is the most effective approach to manage this situation?
- A) Ignore the argument and proceed with the meeting
- B) Escalate the issue to the sponsor
- C) Mediate the situation and encourage both sides to collaborate
- D) Choose one team member's side and move forward

40. According to McGregor's Theory X and Theory Y, which of the following statements best reflects Theory Y management?
- A) Employees are inherently lazy and need constant supervision
- B) Employees are self-motivated and seek responsibility
- C) Employees need financial rewards to perform well
- D) Employees need strict rules to follow

Process Domain

41. A project has an Earned Value (EV) of $80,000, a Planned Value (PV) of $100,000, and an Actual Cost (AC) of $70,000. What is the Schedule Performance Index (SPI)?
- A) 0.8
- B) 1.14
- C) 1.25
- D) 0.7

42. What is the purpose of conducting a "Control Quality" process?
- A) To prevent defects from occurring in project deliverables
- B) To monitor and record the results of executing quality activities
- C) To ensure stakeholder satisfaction with the project scope
- D) To create quality metrics for future projects

43. Which estimating technique uses historical data from similar projects to estimate costs or durations?
- A) Parametric Estimating
- B) Bottom-up Estimating
- C) Analogous Estimating
- D) Three-point Estimating

44. In risk management, what is the key output of the "Identify Risks" process?
- A) Risk Register
- B) Risk Breakdown Structure
- C) Risk Response Plan
- D) Contingency Reserve

45. During which project management process is the work breakdown structure (WBS) created?
- A) Define Scope
- B) Collect Requirements
- C) Plan Scope Management
- D) Create WBS

46. Which of the following is true about critical path activities?
- A) They have the highest risk
- B) They are the longest activities in the project
- C) They must be completed on time to avoid delaying the project
- D) They can be delayed without affecting the project timeline

47. In earned value management, what does it mean if the cost variance (CV) is positive?
- A) The project is over budget
- B) The project is under budget
- C) The project is on budget
- D) The project has no cost variance

48. A project manager must acquire resources for a new project. What process is being performed?

- A) Plan Resource Management
- B) Acquire Resources
- C) Manage Team
- D) Develop Team

49. The project manager is developing the communications management plan. Which of the following factors should be the most important consideration?
- A) Communication technology
- B) The size of the project team
- C) Stakeholder communication requirements
- D) The location of team members

50. During the "Monitor Risks" process, the project manager identifies that a risk response plan is no longer effective. What is the project manager's next step?
- A) Close the risk
- B) Escalate the issue to the project sponsor
- C) Develop a new risk response plan
- D) Ignore the risk and continue with the current plan

Business Environment Domain

51. Which of the following activities is part of project governance?
- A) Managing project risks and issues
- B) Ensuring compliance with organizational policies
- C) Developing the project charter
- D) Approving the project schedule

52. A key component of an organization's governance framework is:
- A) The organizational process assets
- B) The risk management plan
- C) The project charter
- D) The benefits realization plan

53. Which type of contract places the most cost risk on the buyer?
- A) Fixed-price contract

- B) Time and Materials contract
- C) Cost-Reimbursable contract
- D) Cost Plus Fixed Fee contract

54. If a project is terminated early, which of the following should the project manager focus on first?
    - A) Archiving project documents
    - B) Communicating project closure to stakeholders
    - C) Closing procurement contracts
    - D) Completing the final deliverables

55. When aligning a project with the business strategy, what should be the project manager's top priority?
    - A) Ensuring the project deliverables meet technical requirements
    - B) Aligning the project objectives with the organization's goals
    - C) Completing the project within the planned schedule
    - D) Reducing project risks

Agile and Hybrid

56. In agile project management, what does the term "burn-down chart" refer to?
    - A) A chart that tracks project costs over time
    - B) A visual tool used to measure how much work remains in a sprint
    - C) A tool to assign tasks to team members
    - D) A schedule that details project milestones

57. During the sprint planning meeting, the team realizes that the workload is too large for the upcoming sprint. What should the team do?
    - A) Split the workload evenly among all members
    - B) Adjust the sprint goal to a more achievable target
    - C) Add more team members to the sprint
    - D) Cancel the sprint and start over

58. In a hybrid project, which part of the project should be managed using a predictive (waterfall) approach?

- A) Flexible and uncertain tasks
- B) Repetitive and predictable tasks
- C) Tasks that require iterative development
- D) Short-term tasks with unclear outcomes

59. What is the primary responsibility of a Scrum Master in an agile project?
- A) Writing user stories for the product backlog
- B) Prioritizing the work for the development team
- C) Facilitating communication and removing impediments
- D) Approving the work completed by the team

60. What is the most effective way to handle changes in requirements during an agile project?
- A) Reject the changes and stick to the original plan
- B) Freeze requirements at the start of the project
- C) Adjust the backlog and reprioritize based on new requirements
- D) Implement the changes without consulting the team

Ethics and Professional Conduct

61. According to PMI's Code of Ethics, how should a project manager handle conflicts of interest?
- A) Avoid disclosing any conflicts to protect the project
- B) Disclose conflicts of interest to stakeholders and resolve them
- C) Leave the conflict unresolved until the project is complete
- D) Ignore the conflict as long as it doesn't directly affect the project

62. A project manager is aware of a potential legal issue with the project deliverables but has not informed the sponsor. What ethical principle is the project manager violating?
- A) Responsibility
- B) Fairness
- C) Respect
- D) Honesty

63. What is the project manager's responsibility regarding confidential project information?
- A) Share it with the entire project team
- B) Protect confidential information and share it only with authorized individuals
- C) Keep the information secret from stakeholders
- D) Disclose it only to external vendors

64. The project manager receives a complaint from a team member about unethical behavior. What should the project manager do?
- A) Investigate the issue and escalate if necessary
- B) Ignore the issue to avoid conflict
- C) Tell the team member to report the issue themselves
- D) Immediately involve the project sponsor

65. A project manager realizes they have inadvertently left out a key stakeholder during project planning. What is the most ethical way to resolve this?
- A) Notify the stakeholder and update the project plans accordingly
- B) Proceed with the project as planned to avoid delays
- C) Ignore the stakeholder and hope they don't notice
- D) Blame the team for the oversight

66. During project execution, a vendor offers the project manager a valuable gift. According to PMI's Code of Ethics, what is the appropriate action?
- A) Accept the gift if it's under a certain value
- B) Politely refuse the gift and explain the policy
- C) Accept the gift but don't inform anyone
- D) Accept the gift only if the vendor is critical to the project

Answers for Set 2 (Questions 34–66)

34. D
35. C
36. B
37. B
38. C
39. C
40. B
41. A
42. B
43. C
44. A
45. D
46. C
47. B
48. B
49. C
50. C
51. B
52. D
53. C
54. C
55. B
56. B
57. B
58. B
59. C
60. C
61. B
62. D
63. B
64. A
65. A
66. B

PMP Exam - Set 3 (Questions 67-99)

People Domain

67. A team member misses several key meetings and falls behind on their assigned tasks. What should the project manager do first?
- A) Report the issue to the sponsor
- B) Escalate the issue to HR
- C) Meet privately with the team member to understand the problem
- D) Reassign the team member's tasks to others

68. Which of the following factors contributes most to team performance and project success?
- A) Technical skills of the team members
- B) Effective communication and collaboration among team members
- C) The number of team members
- D) Use of project management software

69. In which scenario is a servant leadership style most effective?
- A) A high-performing team that requires little guidance
- B) A newly formed team that needs strict oversight
- C) An agile team that values self-organization and collaboration
- D) A team with low motivation that needs constant direction

70. A project manager notices that a team member is struggling with their workload. What is the best course of action?
- A) Assign more tasks to other team members
- B) Encourage the team member to work overtime
- C) Provide support and resources to help the team member succeed
- D) Criticize the team member for underperformance

71. In the Tuckman model of team development, what is the best description of the "Norming" stage?
- A) Team members are forming initial relationships and learning about the project
- B) Conflicts arise, and roles are established within the team

- C) The team begins to work more cohesively, with stronger collaboration and cooperation
- D) The team reaches peak performance and works efficiently with minimal supervision

---

Process Domain

72. A project's cost performance index (CPI) is 0.8, and the schedule performance index (SPI) is 0.9. What do these indices indicate about the project?
    - A) The project is under budget and ahead of schedule
    - B) The project is over budget and ahead of schedule
    - C) The project is over budget and behind schedule
    - D) The project is on budget and on schedule

73. The project manager is conducting a root cause analysis to identify the underlying reasons for repeated quality issues. Which tool is most appropriate for this task?
    - A) Pareto Chart
    - B) Fishbone Diagram (Ishikawa Diagram)
    - C) Control Chart
    - D) Scatter Diagram

74. During the Monitor Risks process, a new risk is identified that could significantly affect project success. What should the project manager do next?
    - A) Ignore the risk until it occurs
    - B) Add the risk to the risk register and develop a risk response plan
    - C) Escalate the risk to the project sponsor
    - D) Cancel the project

75. The project manager must update the project schedule. Which tool or technique is best suited for this task?
    - A) Expert Judgment
    - B) Network Diagram
    - C) Gantt Chart
    - D) Project Charter

76. In a project using earned value management (EVM), the project's earned value (EV) is $50,000, the planned value (PV) is $60,000, and the actual cost (AC) is $55,000. What is the project's cost variance (CV)?
- A) $5,000
- B) -$5,000
- C) $10,000
- D) -$10,000

77. Which of the following is not a characteristic of a Work Breakdown Structure (WBS)?
- A) It provides a hierarchical structure of work packages
- B) It focuses on deliverables
- C) It includes cost estimates for each task
- D) It helps identify all project work

78. What is the primary purpose of Perform Qualitative Risk Analysis?
- A) To rank project risks based on probability and impact
- B) To assign a numerical value to the impact of each risk
- C) To identify new risks that have not been previously considered
- D) To create detailed risk response strategies

79. The project manager is creating a cost management plan for a complex project. What is the most appropriate cost estimating technique to use when detailed project information is not yet available?
- A) Parametric Estimating
- B) Analogous Estimating
- C) Bottom-up Estimating
- D) Three-point Estimating

80. A project manager is managing a project in a hybrid environment, where part of the project uses predictive techniques and part uses agile. Which approach should the project manager take to ensure the project's success?
- A) Use only predictive techniques throughout the project
- B) Combine the best practices of both predictive and agile methods
- C) Use agile techniques only during the planning phase
- D) Use agile techniques only when the project is behind schedule

Business Environment Domain

81. A project manager is responsible for ensuring the project complies with new government regulations. What should the project manager do first?
    - A) Perform an impact analysis to assess the effect of the regulation on the project
    - B) Notify all stakeholders of the new regulation
    - C) Update the risk register with the new regulation
    - D) Cancel the project if the regulation is too restrictive

82. The project is nearing completion, and the project manager is focusing on benefits realization. What is the goal of this process?
    - A) Completing the final deliverables
    - B) Ensuring that the project outcomes deliver the intended business value
    - C) Obtaining final approval from the sponsor
    - D) Closing all procurement contracts

83. A project manager is working in an organization with a weak matrix structure. What challenge is the project manager likely to face in this environment?
    - A) Having little authority over resources and decision-making
    - B) Managing multiple projects simultaneously
    - C) Dealing with high levels of bureaucracy
    - D) Handling too many stakeholders

84. In a cost-reimbursable contract, what is the biggest risk for the buyer?
    - A) The project may exceed the planned budget
    - B) The seller may not deliver the agreed-upon product
    - C) The project may finish ahead of schedule
    - D) The project scope may change

85. Which of the following factors is most important when aligning a project with the organization's strategic goals?
    - A) Adherence to the project schedule
    - B) Alignment of the project objectives with the organization's long-term goals
    - C) Minimizing project risks

- D) Securing stakeholder approval

Agile and Hybrid

86. A Scrum Master notices that team members are not adhering to the agreed-upon agile practices. How should the Scrum Master address this?
    - A) Escalate the issue to senior management
    - B) Implement a new set of agile practices immediately
    - C) Facilitate a team discussion to revisit and reinforce the agile practices
    - D) Ignore the issue and let the team self-correct

87. During a sprint retrospective, the agile team identifies several areas for improvement. What should the team do next?
    - A) Stop the current sprint and implement the improvements immediately
    - B) Add the improvements to the product backlog
    - C) Adjust the sprint plan to include the improvements in the next sprint
    - D) Conduct a root cause analysis to determine the reason for the issues

88. In an agile project, which artifact provides a visual representation of the remaining work in a sprint?
    - A) Product Backlog
    - B) Sprint Backlog
    - C) Burn-down Chart
    - D) Kanban Board

89. Which of the following is not a typical agile principle?
    - A) Responding to change over following a plan
    - B) Comprehensive documentation over working software
    - C) Customer collaboration over contract negotiation
    - D) Individuals and interactions over processes and tools

90. What is the role of a Product Owner in Scrum?
    - A) Writing code for the product
    - B) Removing impediments for the team
    - C) Prioritizing the product backlog

- D) Facilitating sprint reviews

Ethics and Professional Conduct

91. A project manager realizes they accidentally shared confidential project information with an unauthorized stakeholder. According to PMI's Code of Ethics, what should the project manager do?
    - A) Apologize and ask the stakeholder to keep the information confidential
    - B) Report the incident to the sponsor and correct the mistake
    - C) Ignore the issue as long as no harm was done
    - D) Reprimand the stakeholder for accepting the information

92. According to PMI's Code of Ethics, which of the following best demonstrates respect in a project environment?
    - A) Taking responsibility for project success
    - B) Treating all stakeholders with fairness and dignity
    - C) Reporting unethical behavior in a timely manner
    - D) Ensuring all team members follow the project plan exactly

93. A project manager is offered a significant gift by a vendor, which is against the company's policy. What is the most ethical action the project manager should take?
    - A) Accept the gift and not disclose it
    - B) Politely refuse the gift and explain the company policy
    - C) Accept the gift if it benefits the project
    - D) Keep the gift but avoid future dealings with the vendor

94. A project manager is struggling to maintain team morale due to tight deadlines. What is the most ethical course of action?
    - A) Encourage the team to work overtime to meet deadlines
    - B) Report the issue to the sponsor and propose a timeline adjustment
    - C) Dismiss team concerns to maintain focus on project delivery
    - D) Assign additional tasks to the high-performing team members

95. A team member reports a potential conflict of interest involving another team member. What is the project manager's first responsibility?
- A) Investigate the situation and resolve it based on company policies
- B) Report the conflict to senior management
- C) Ignore the conflict to avoid disrupting the project
- D) Encourage the team member to address the issue directly

96. During project execution, a vendor approaches the project manager with confidential information about a competitor. According to PMI's Code of Ethics, what should the project manager do?
- A) Accept the information to gain a competitive advantage
- B) Report the vendor to their supervisor for unethical conduct
- C) Refuse the information and report the incident to the project sponsor
- D) Keep the information confidential and use it discreetly

97. The project manager receives confidential information that could impact the project's success. How should the project manager handle this information?
- A) Disclose the information to all team members
- B) Share the information with only the sponsor and relevant stakeholders
- C) Ignore the information to avoid complicating the project
- D) Make the information public to prevent rumors

98. A project manager is under pressure to meet project deadlines but discovers a significant risk that could affect the timeline. What should the project manager do?
- A) Notify stakeholders and adjust the project plan accordingly
- B) Ignore the risk to avoid alarming the stakeholders
- C) Continue working without informing anyone
- D) Delay the project and avoid discussing the risk

99. A project manager has a personal relationship with a key stakeholder, which could influence project decisions. What is the project manager's ethical responsibility?
- A) Continue managing the project but avoid disclosing the relationship
- B) Disclose the relationship to relevant stakeholders and resolve any conflicts of interest
- C) Use the relationship to gain an advantage for the project

- D) Step down from the project to avoid conflicts

Answers for Set 3 (Questions 67-99)

67. C
68. B
69. C
70. C
71. C
72. C
73. B
74. B
75. C
76. B
77. C
78. A
79. B
80. B
81. A
82. B
83. A
84. A
85. B
86. C
87. C
88. C
89. B
90. C
91. B
92. B
93. B
94. B
95. A
96. C
97. B
98. A
99. B

PART B

PMP Exam – Set 1 (Questions 1-33)

People Domain

1. What is the best approach to managing a high-power, high-interest stakeholder?
    - A) Keep them informed
    - B) Manage them closely
    - C) Monitor with minimal effort
    - D) Keep them satisfied

2. A project manager needs to address low team performance. According to Herzberg's Two-Factor Theory, which factor should be improved to motivate the team?
    - A) Hygiene factors
    - B) Motivating factors
    - C) Performance appraisals
    - D) Financial bonuses

3. A team member is consistently late in delivering their work. What should the project manager do first?
    - A) Replace the team member
    - B) Assign the work to another team member
    - C) Meet privately with the team member to understand the issue
    - D) Escalate the issue to the sponsor

4. In agile projects, who is responsible for defining and prioritizing the product backlog?
    - A) Project Manager
    - B) Scrum Master
    - C) Development Team
    - D) Product Owner

5. Which conflict resolution technique emphasizes the importance of collaboration for mutual benefits?
    - A) Forcing

- B) Avoiding
- C) Collaborating
- D) Compromising

6. During the project execution, the team reports that a critical task will be delayed. How should the project manager respond?
    - A) Reassign the task to another team member
    - B) Revise the project schedule
    - C) Ignore the delay
    - D) Escalate the issue to the project sponsor

7. When working with a diverse team, what is the most important consideration for the project manager?
    - A) Managing conflicts effectively
    - B) Focusing on individual performance
    - C) Ensuring mutual respect and inclusivity
    - D) Using authoritative leadership styles

8. What leadership style is most effective in an agile project environment?
    - A) Autocratic
    - B) Servant Leadership
    - C) Transformational Leadership
    - D) Transactional

9. A project manager needs to assign roles in a new project. What is the most important factor to consider when assigning team members?
    - A) Their interest in the project
    - B) Their availability
    - C) Their skill sets
    - D) Their geographic location

10. When providing feedback to team members, what is the most effective approach?
    - A) Give feedback in a public setting
    - B) Use constructive criticism and specific examples

- C) Praise all team members equally
- D) Avoid giving feedback to prevent conflict

Process Domain

11. A project manager wants to identify key deliverables and their dependencies. Which tool should they use?
    - A) Gantt Chart
    - B) Work Breakdown Structure (WBS)
    - C) Stakeholder Register
    - D) Risk Register

12. What is the purpose of the "Control Costs" process?
    - A) Estimating project costs
    - B) Defining the project budget
    - C) Monitoring project expenditures and controlling cost variances
    - D) Closing project costs

13. The project manager needs to analyze the impacts of potential risks on cost and schedule. Which analysis technique should they use?
    - A) Qualitative Risk Analysis
    - B) Quantitative Risk Analysis
    - C) Sensitivity Analysis
    - D) SWOT Analysis

14. What is the first step in developing a Risk Management Plan?
    - A) Identify risks
    - B) Plan risk responses
    - C) Perform risk analysis
    - D) Develop risk thresholds

15. In earned value management, which formula is used to calculate cost variance (CV)?
    - A) CV = EV − AC
    - B) CV = EV − PV

- C) CV = AC - PV
- D) CV = BAC - EV

16. If a project's Schedule Performance Index (SPI) is 0.75, what does this indicate?
    - A) The project is behind schedule
    - B) The project is ahead of schedule
    - C) The project is under budget
    - D) The project is over budget

17. A team is creating the project's detailed schedule. Which tool is most appropriate for determining the critical path?
    - A) Gantt Chart
    - B) Critical Path Method (CPM)
    - C) Monte Carlo Simulation
    - D) Risk Breakdown Structure

18. During project planning, which document outlines how changes will be managed in the project?
    - A) Scope Management Plan
    - B) Change Control Plan
    - C) Risk Management Plan
    - D) Communications Management Plan

19. A project's actual cost (AC) is $100,000, earned value (EV) is $90,000, and planned value (PV) is $95,000. What is the cost performance index (CPI)?
    - A) 1.1
    - B) 0.9
    - C) 1.05
    - D) 0.95

20. The project manager is performing a stakeholder analysis to prioritize stakeholders. What tool is commonly used to map stakeholders based on power and interest?
    - A) RACI Matrix
    - B) Stakeholder Register

- C) Power/Interest Grid
- D) Risk Register

Business Environment Domain

21. A project manager is working on a project that must comply with new industry regulations. What should the project manager do first?
    - A) Ignore the regulation and continue as planned
    - B) Update the risk register to include the regulation
    - C) Adjust the project scope to comply with the regulation
    - D) Escalate the issue to the sponsor

22. Which type of contract is typically used when the buyer wants to transfer the maximum risk to the seller?
    - A) Cost-Reimbursable Contract
    - B) Time and Materials Contract
    - C) Fixed-Price Contract
    - D) Cost Plus Incentive Fee Contract

23. A project is terminated early due to shifting business priorities. What is the project manager's first responsibility?
    - A) Perform a root cause analysis
    - B) Notify stakeholders and initiate project closure procedures
    - C) Reallocate resources to other projects
    - D) Archive project documentation

24. In a projectized organization, what is the project manager's level of authority?
    - A) Low
    - B) Moderate
    - C) High
    - D) Minimal

25. Which of the following is a primary objective of benefits realization?
    - A) Delivering project scope within budget
    - B) Ensuring the project's deliverables align with business objectives

- C) Completing the project on time
- D) Ensuring regulatory compliance

Agile and Hybrid

26. In agile, what is the primary responsibility of the Scrum Master?
    - A) Prioritizing the backlog
    - B) Assigning tasks to the team
    - C) Removing impediments and facilitating team meetings
    - D) Defining the project scope

27. During the sprint retrospective, the agile team focuses on:
    - A) Demonstrating completed work to stakeholders
    - B) Identifying process improvements for future sprints
    - C) Refining the backlog
    - D) Assigning tasks for the next sprint

28. What is the key characteristic of time-boxed sprints in agile?
    - A) Sprints have no fixed duration
    - B) Sprints have a fixed duration, typically 1-4 weeks
    - C) Work can continue until all tasks are complete
    - D) Only the Product Owner determines sprint length

29. In a hybrid project, which approach is best for managing work that is repetitive and predictable?
    - A) Agile approach
    - B) Predictive (Waterfall) approach
    - C) Kanban approach
    - D) Scrum approach

30. A team using Scrum is unable to complete all the stories in a sprint. What should they do?
    - A) Carry the incomplete stories into the next sprint
    - B) Extend the sprint until all tasks are completed
    - C) Cancel the sprint and start over

- D) Assign the stories to another team

Ethics and Professional Conduct

31. A project manager learns that a key stakeholder has been excluded from key decisions. What should the project manager do?
    - A) Ignore the issue to avoid conflict
    - B) Update the stakeholder register and include the stakeholder in future communications
    - C) Report the oversight to the sponsor
    - D) Continue the project as planned

32. A vendor offers the project manager a gift during the project. What should the project manager do according to PMI's Code of Ethics?
    - A) Accept the gift if it benefits the project
    - B) Politely decline the gift and explain the organization's policy
    - C) Accept the gift and report it to the sponsor
    - D) Accept the gift and keep it confidential

33. A project manager is aware that a team member is involved in unethical practices. What should the project manager do?
    - A) Investigate and report the unethical practices to the appropriate authority
    - B) Ignore the issue
    - C) Discuss the issue with the team privately
    - D) Allow the sponsor to handle the situation

Answers for Set 1 (Questions 1-33)

1. B
2. B
3. C
4. D
5. C
6. B
7. C
8. B
9. C
10. B
11. B
12. C
13. B
14. A
15. A
16. A
17. B
18. B
19. B
20. C
21. B
22. C
23. B
24. C
25. B
26. C
27. B
28. B
29. B
30. A
31. B
32. B
33. A

PMP Exam - Set 2 (Questions 34-66)

People Domain

34. A project manager notices that one team member is underperforming due to personal issues. What should the project manager do first?
- A) Escalate the issue to HR
- B) Reassign the team member's tasks
- C) Meet with the team member privately to offer support and discuss solutions
- D) Ignore the issue and hope it resolves

35. A project team is consistently missing deadlines due to miscommunication. What is the best action for the project manager to take?
- A) Increase the frequency of team meetings
- B) Replace team members
- C) Implement a more structured communication plan
- D) Reduce the workload

36. Which leadership style is most effective when managing an experienced, self-motivated team?
- A) Laissez-faire
- B) Autocratic
- C) Democratic
- D) Transactional

37. When managing a global project team, what should the project manager consider to ensure effective communication?
- A) Technical expertise of the team
- B) Cultural differences and time zones
- C) Only project priorities
- D) Team members' education levels

38. A key stakeholder requests a major scope change mid-project. What should the project manager do?
- A) Implement the change immediately

- B) Analyze the impact of the change and follow the change control process
- C) Reject the request to avoid delays
- D) Forward the request to the project sponsor

39. A team member consistently completes tasks ahead of schedule. How should the project manager handle this situation?
- A) Increase the team member's workload
- B) Praise the team member and acknowledge their efforts
- C) Assign the team member to mentor others
- D) Reduce the team member's workload to balance the pace

40. Which of the following is true about the Tuckman model of team development?
- A) The Storming phase occurs after the Performing phase
- B) Teams in the Performing stage are at their most productive
- C) The Norming phase involves the least amount of conflict
- D) The team disbands in the Storming phase

Process Domain

41. A project manager needs to determine the root cause of recurring project delays. Which tool should they use?
- A) Control Chart
- B) Fishbone Diagram (Ishikawa Diagram)
- C) Pareto Chart
- D) Monte Carlo Simulation

42. The critical path is important because:
- A) It shows the path with the most tasks
- B) It represents the longest sequence of activities that determine the project's duration
- C) It has the highest risk of failure
- D) It allows flexibility for delays

43. A project manager realizes that a key deliverable is at risk of being delayed. What is the best action to take first?

- A) Inform the sponsor immediately
- B) Perform an impact analysis on the project schedule
- C) Shift resources from other tasks to speed up the deliverable
- D) Extend the project timeline

44. During the Control Quality process, the project manager finds that 7% of deliverables do not meet quality standards. What should they do next?
- A) Rework the deliverables to meet the standards
- B) Ignore the issue and proceed
- C) Reject the deliverables
- D) Escalate the issue to the project sponsor

45. In a project, earned value (EV) is $70,000, actual cost (AC) is $80,000, and planned value (PV) is $75,000. What is the cost variance (CV)?
- A) -$10,000
- B) $10,000
- C) -$5,000
- D) $5,000

46. Which project document identifies the roles and responsibilities of each team member?
- A) Responsibility Assignment Matrix (RAM)
- B) RACI Matrix
- C) Communications Management Plan
- D) Organizational Breakdown Structure (OBS)

47. During the Plan Procurement Management process, the project manager needs to determine how many resources are required. What is the best estimating technique to use if detailed information is limited?
- A) Bottom-Up Estimating
- B) Analogous Estimating
- C) Parametric Estimating
- D) Three-Point Estimating

48. In earned value management, which formula is used to calculate Schedule Variance (SV)?
   - A) SV = EV - PV
   - B) SV = AC - EV
   - C) SV = PV - AC
   - D) SV = BAC - EV

49. A team is evaluating the risks associated with each task in the project. What tool or technique is used to rank risks based on probability and impact?
   - A) Sensitivity Analysis
   - B) Pareto Analysis
   - C) Qualitative Risk Analysis
   - D) Quantitative Risk Analysis

50. A project team is conducting a brainstorming session to identify new risks. What risk management process is the team performing?
   - A) Monitor Risks
   - B) Identify Risks
   - C) Perform Qualitative Risk Analysis
   - D) Plan Risk Responses

Business Environment Domain

51. During a project review, the sponsor suggests canceling the project due to a lack of alignment with business objectives. What should the project manager do first?
   - A) Proceed with the project until given formal approval to stop
   - B) Perform a detailed analysis to determine whether the project is aligned with current business objectives
   - C) Cancel the project immediately
   - D) Delay the project to re-evaluate

52. A project is transitioning into its closure phase. What should the project manager focus on to ensure benefits realization?
   - A) Completing deliverables on time
   - B) Ensuring the project outcomes provide long-term business value
   - C) Getting final stakeholder approval

- D) Reducing project costs

53. Which type of contract is used when there is uncertainty about the project's cost but a price ceiling is necessary to limit risk to the buyer?
    - A) Fixed-Price Contract
    - B) Cost Plus Fixed Fee Contract
    - C) Time and Materials Contract
    - D) Cost Plus Incentive Fee Contract

54. A weak matrix organizational structure typically results in:
    - A) High authority for the project manager
    - B) Shared authority between the project manager and functional manager
    - C) The project manager having minimal authority
    - D) Full authority for the project sponsor

55. Which document captures project details, including assumptions, constraints, and high-level risks?
    - A) Project Charter
    - B) Project Management Plan
    - C) Stakeholder Register
    - D) Risk Register

Agile and Hybrid

56. In agile, what is the purpose of a sprint review?
    - A) Discussing issues encountered during the sprint
    - B) Refining the backlog for future sprints
    - C) Demonstrating the work completed to stakeholders
    - D) Conducting root cause analysis

57. The team is discussing incremental delivery in an agile project. What does this term mean?
    - A) Delivering the entire product at the end of the project
    - B) Delivering the product in phases or iterations
    - C) Delivering only non-functional aspects of the product first

- D) Delivering half of the project scope initially

58. During a sprint, the agile team realizes that they won't complete all the tasks by the end of the sprint. What is the most appropriate action?
- A) Extend the sprint to complete the remaining tasks
- B) Stop the sprint and start a new one
- C) Carry incomplete tasks to the next sprint
- D) Reassign tasks to other team members

59. What does continuous integration refer to in agile projects?
- A) Integrating stakeholder feedback after each release
- B) Regularly integrating code into a shared repository to detect issues early
- C) Continuous involvement of team members in all project activities
- D) Regularly updating project documentation

60. Which of the following best describes the role of a Product Owner in Scrum?
- A) Managing the development team
- B) Prioritizing and refining the product backlog
- C) Managing risks and issues
- D) Removing impediments

Ethics and Professional Conduct

61. A project manager discovers that one of the team members has been misrepresenting project data. What should the project manager do according to PMI's Code of Ethics?
- A) Ignore the issue to avoid team conflict
- B) Investigate the situation and address the issue with the team member
- C) Escalate the issue to HR immediately
- D) Report the issue to the project sponsor

62. A stakeholder requests confidential information about a competitor's project. How should the project manager respond?
- A) Refuse to share the information and explain the ethical guidelines
- B) Share the information only with key stakeholders

- C) Ignore the request
- D) Escalate the request to the sponsor

63. A team member approaches the project manager about unethical practices occurring in the project. What should the project manager do?
- A) Investigate and address the unethical practices
- B) Dismiss the concern if it doesn't affect project deliverables
- C) Ask the team member to handle it themselves
- D) Ignore the issue to avoid conflict

64. A vendor offers a project manager a gift during project execution. What is the most appropriate action according to PMI's Code of Ethics?
- A) Politely decline the gift and explain the company policy
- B) Accept the gift and inform the sponsor
- C) Accept the gift and keep it confidential
- D) Accept the gift if it benefits the project

65. A project manager notices that team members are underperforming due to excessive workload. What is the most ethical course of action?
- A) Encourage the team to work overtime
- B) Discuss the issue with the sponsor and suggest reducing the workload
- C) Ignore the issue to meet project deadlines
- D) Assign additional tasks to the high-performing team members

66. A project manager is aware of a potential conflict of interest involving a key decision-maker. What is the project manager's responsibility?
- A) Disclose the conflict of interest to stakeholders and take action to resolve it
- B) Ignore the conflict to maintain focus on the project
- C) Escalate the issue to senior management immediately
- D) Continue managing the project without disclosure

Answers for Set 2 (Questions 34–66)

34. C
35. C
36. A
37. B
38. B
39. B
40. B
41. B
42. B
43. B
44. A
45. A
46. A
47. B
48. A
49. C
50. B
51. B
52. B
53. D
54. C
55. A
56. C
57. B
58. C
59. B
60. B
61. B
62. A
63. A
64. A
65. B
66. A

PMP Exam - Set 3 (Questions 67-99)

People Domain

67. A project manager is leading a team with significant differences in work styles and cultural backgrounds. What is the most effective strategy to foster collaboration?
- A) Encourage team members to work independently
- B) Enforce a uniform work style for all team members
- C) Promote open communication and mutual respect for differences
- D) Focus only on technical skills and ignore cultural differences

68. A project team member suggests a new tool that could enhance productivity. What should the project manager do?
- A) Reject the suggestion to avoid scope creep
- B) Analyze the potential impact of the tool and present it to the team
- C) Ignore the suggestion to maintain focus on current processes
- D) Implement the tool immediately

69. A senior stakeholder is unhappy with the progress of a project. How should the project manager handle this?
- A) Escalate the issue to the project sponsor
- B) Address the stakeholder's concerns and provide regular updates
- C) Avoid the stakeholder until project progress improves
- D) Focus on the team's internal processes and ignore the stakeholder's concerns

70. When managing a virtual team, what is the most important practice for effective team management?
- A) Minimizing communication to reduce distractions
- B) Focusing on individual performance reviews
- C) Scheduling regular video meetings to maintain engagement
- D) Limiting collaboration to avoid confusion

71. A project team is in the Norming stage of the Tuckman model. What characterizes this phase?

- A) Increased conflict and disagreements
- B) Team members working collaboratively with minimal supervision
- C) Formation of the team and initial relationship building
- D) Team members challenging the authority of the project manager

---

Process Domain

72. A project is facing frequent scope changes requested by stakeholders. What should the project manager do to maintain control?
- A) Deny all scope changes
- B) Implement changes immediately without analysis
- C) Follow the formal change control process for all change requests
- D) Avoid informing stakeholders about the impact of changes

73. A project manager is working on a project with a tight budget. Which of the following processes helps ensure that the project stays within budget?
- A) Plan Resource Management
- B) Control Costs
- C) Develop Schedule
- D) Perform Qualitative Risk Analysis

74. A project manager uses a Monte Carlo simulation to assess the impact of risk on the project schedule. What type of risk analysis is this?
- A) Qualitative Risk Analysis
- B) Quantitative Risk Analysis
- C) Risk Response Planning
- D) Risk Register Update

75. The project manager is in the Direct and Manage Project Work process. What is the main focus of this process?
- A) Tracking project progress and performance
- B) Executing the work defined in the project management plan to achieve objectives
- C) Closing project contracts
- D) Defining the project scope

76. A project manager wants to ensure that project activities are completed in the correct sequence. Which of the following tools is most appropriate for this?
- A) Monte Carlo Analysis
- B) Network Diagram
- C) Stakeholder Register
- D) Resource Histogram

77. During project execution, a team member reports an unexpected risk that was not identified during planning. What should the project manager do?
- A) Ignore the risk if it hasn't occurred yet
- B) Add the risk to the risk register and develop a response plan
- C) Escalate the risk to the sponsor immediately
- D) Reassign tasks to other team members

78. A project is delayed, and the project manager uses fast tracking to bring it back on schedule. What is a key risk of this technique?
- A) Increased project costs
- B) Reduced project quality
- C) Increased scope creep
- D) Increased project risks due to overlapping tasks

79. During Monitor Communications, what is the primary focus of the project manager?
- A) Ensuring stakeholders receive the information they need in a timely manner
- B) Analyzing stakeholder concerns
- C) Revising the project schedule
- D) Closing communication channels to prevent distractions

80. A project manager is conducting a performance review to assess the project's progress. Which of the following is the best tool to use?
- A) Resource Breakdown Structure (RBS)
- B) Gantt Chart
- C) Project Charter
- D) Earned Value Management (EVM)

Business Environment Domain

81. Which document provides formal authorization to initiate a project?
    - A) Project Charter
    - B) Project Management Plan
    - C) Scope Management Plan
    - D) Statement of Work

82. A project manager is responsible for ensuring that the project outcomes align with business goals. What process helps ensure this?
    - A) Develop Project Charter
    - B) Benefits Realization
    - C) Control Scope
    - D) Close Project or Phase

83. Which type of contract involves paying the seller for allowable costs plus a fee for achieving specific performance targets?
    - A) Time and Materials Contract
    - B) Fixed-Price Contract
    - C) Cost Plus Incentive Fee (CPIF) Contract
    - D) Cost-Reimbursable Contract

84. A project manager is working in an organization with a strong matrix structure. What is the project manager's level of authority in this environment?
    - A) Low
    - B) High
    - C) Moderate
    - D) Minimal

85. During project execution, a government regulation changes and impacts the project's deliverables. What should the project manager do first?
    - A) Ignore the regulation since the project has already started
    - B) Update the project risk register and communicate the impact to stakeholders
    - C) Cancel the project
    - D) Request more funding to comply with the regulation

Agile and Hybrid

86. In a Scrum team, who is responsible for ensuring that the team follows agile principles and removes obstacles?
    - A) Product Owner
    - B) Scrum Master
    - C) Project Manager
    - D) Team Lead

87. What is the key difference between incremental and iterative delivery in agile projects?
    - A) Incremental focuses on delivering a part of the product in stages, while iterative focuses on refining the product through repeated cycles
    - B) Incremental delivers the entire product at the end, while iterative delivers it in small parts
    - C) Iterative allows for flexible changes, while incremental does not
    - D) Incremental and iterative delivery are the same

88. In agile, what is the purpose of a sprint backlog?
    - A) To list all tasks for the entire project
    - B) To track defects and issues
    - C) To define the work to be completed during a sprint
    - D) To prioritize features for future releases

89. What is timeboxing in agile?
    - A) Limiting the duration of meetings or activities to a set time period
    - B) Scheduling work without any time constraints
    - C) Extending the timeline when more tasks need to be completed
    - D) Prioritizing tasks based on importance rather than time

90. The product owner wants to change the scope of the project mid-sprint. What is the correct course of action?
    - A) Implement the changes immediately
    - B) Add the change request to the product backlog for future consideration
    - C) Restart the sprint with the new scope
    - D) Escalate the issue to the Scrum Master

Ethics and Professional Conduct

91. A project manager is pressured to overlook a safety issue in order to meet a deadline. What is the most ethical course of action?
    - A) Address the safety issue immediately, even if it impacts the schedule
    - B) Meet the deadline and address the issue later
    - C) Ignore the safety issue to meet stakeholder expectations
    - D) Report the issue to the project sponsor but take no immediate action

92. A team member approaches the project manager with concerns about another team member's unethical behavior. What should the project manager do?
    - A) Investigate and address the unethical behavior
    - B) Ignore the concern to avoid team conflict
    - C) Reassign the team member to another project
    - D) Escalate the issue to HR without investigation

93. According to PMI's Code of Ethics, how should a project manager handle confidential information?
    - A) Share it with the entire project team
    - B) Protect it and share it only with authorized individuals
    - C) Disclose it to stakeholders as needed
    - D) Ignore confidentiality requirements if the project benefits

94. A stakeholder offers the project manager an expensive gift during a critical phase of the project. What should the project manager do according to PMI's Code of Ethics?
    - A) Accept the gift and inform the team
    - B) Politely refuse the gift and explain the organization's policy
    - C) Accept the gift to maintain good stakeholder relations
    - D) Accept the gift if it helps the project

95. A project manager realizes they accidentally excluded a key stakeholder from important communications. What should the project manager do?
    - A) Ignore the issue to avoid delays
    - B) Update the stakeholder and provide necessary information

- C) Blame the project team for the oversight
- D) Escalate the issue to senior management

96. A vendor offers confidential information about a competitor's project to the project manager. What is the most appropriate action according to PMI's Code of Ethics?
- A) Accept the information and use it to the project's advantage
- B) Refuse the information and report the incident
- C) Accept the information but keep it confidential
- D) Escalate the issue to the project sponsor

97. During a project, a team member requests that the project manager sign off on work that has not yet been completed. What should the project manager do?
- A) Refuse to sign off until the work is fully completed
- B) Sign off to keep the project on track
- C) Escalate the issue to the sponsor
- D) Ignore the request and proceed with the project

98. A project manager receives a complaint about favoritism toward one team member. What is the most ethical response?
- A) Ignore the complaint to avoid conflict
- B) Investigate the complaint and address it if necessary
- C) Reassign the team member to avoid the issue
- D) Dismiss the complaint as baseless

99. A project manager has personal connections with a vendor bidding for a contract. What is the ethical course of action?
- A) Disclose the personal connection and remove themselves from the decision-making process
- B) Award the contract to the vendor due to their relationship
- C) Ignore the personal connection and proceed with the vendor
- D) Keep the connection private but continue to evaluate the vendor

Answers for Set 3 (Questions 67-99)

67. C
68. B
69. B
70. C
71. B
72. C
73. B
74. B
75. B
76. B
77. B
78. D
79. A
80. D
81. A
82. B
83. C
84. B
85. B
86. B
87. A
88. C
89. A
90. B
91. A
92. A
93. B
94. B
95. B
96. B
97. A
98. B
99. A

www.ingramcontent.com/pod-product-compliance
Lightning Source LLC
Chambersburg PA
CBHW081020240526
45471CB00018B/3885